Called Out

Paul Krause

Copyright

Copyright © 2011 - Paul Krause

Cover Image: Reistlin Magere © Copyright Shutterstock Images LLC. Editing Credit: Melody Karpinski and Katie Krause Formating Thanks to Joelle Lawyer

Please note that certain pronouns relating to Father, Son and Holy Spirit were capitalized and may differ from some publishers' styles.

Also take note that the name of satan and related names are not capitalized. We choose not to acknowledge him, regardless of violating grammatical rules.

Called Out Publications
San Diego, Ca 92117

ISBN-10- 0985021829
ISBN-13-978-0-9850218-2-5

www.CALLEDOUTMIN.com

ACKNOWLEDGEMENTS

Above all things and people, I owe Jesus my gratitude. Thank you God for saving me, using me, and giving me beautiful things in place of my ashes. I also want to Honor my family. To my beautiful wife Katie Krause, thank you for all your love. Only God knows all you put into this book, can't wait to read all the books you will write! My brothers, friends, and partners in Revival: Chad Krause, Bryan Mielke, Eddie Brown, Kris Kildosher, Nick Thornhill and Chad Dedmon. To everyone mentioned in this book, thank you for being a part of God's amazing redemptive plan for this world. Special mention to Bryan Mielke, Brett Mielke, Jordyn Osburn, Lauren Lierly, Ryan Mcdonald, Nate Parker and all the others in called out ministries who shared this story with me, you are all my heros. Thank you Melody Karpinski and Joelle Lawyer for all your work on this manuscript. Last but not least, thanks to all of the Spiritual Fathers and Mothers who have lovingly sowed into my life. Thank you to Mark, Debra, George, Heidi, Tiger, Patricia, Rob, and Guy. You have all changed my life forever. And through this book, I pray you will touch many others.

Table of Contents

Credits

Foreword

Called Out 11

Ekklessia 15

Discipling Nations 23

Clothed with Power 31

True Religion 51

A Wedding Story 57

Reformation of Reconciliation 65

Five Fold Ministry of God 73

God's Design 79

Room for Jesus 93

God's Government 99

Catching the Fire 107

About the Author 115

Foreword

I confess I have had many quorums with writing a book. Among them, I simply don't like writing that much. God has taken me through a series of encounters that led me to understanding His will for this book. Hopefully, in sharing with you some of the process, you may better understand the heart and purpose of this book.

When I was 19 years old, God spoke to me in a very soft, yet clearly discernible voice and told me, "I want you to write a book entitled *Called Out*." At the time I had no idea what this meant, but generally thought it was a cool name. A year later I slowly began a book in obedience, though I didn't know what it was about. Later, in Greek class at Bible College, I learned that Called Out was the literal translation of the word "Church." This revelation sent me spiraling down a journey of what it is to be a part of this thing we call "church."

After much of the book was written, I found myself very discouraged, not knowing if a 22 year old could possibly have anything of worth to say to such a broad audience on such an important topic. I was sitting in a pastors meeting one day with some of my heroes including Rolland Baker and Chad Dedmon. There was also a guy named Shawn Bolz who I had never met, but I heard he was well known for hearing the voice of God. After lunch Shawn stood up saying that he had some words from the Lord. He looked at me and my wife Katie (we had only been married a month) and said, "You guys are mothers and fathers. You may feel young but God is making you a mother and father to raise up mothers and fathers even at a young age. He is teaching you about purity in the Church, and there are some books that are going to come out of this. You may feel like it is incomplete or hasn't set, but you need to give away what you have. The whole world needs to hear about these books." At the end of the day, I just want to be obedient. God bless your Bride with the purity and spotlessness that is Her inheritance!

Called Out

"But you are a chosen race, a royal priesthood,
a holy nation, a people for his own possession,
that you may proclaim the excellencies of him
who called you out of darkness into his
marvelous light."
~1 Peter 2:9

When I think of being called out, it reminds me of my childhood. The times when you're sitting in class and the teacher would call on you to speak.   If you were ready, you would sit eagerly in anticipation, hoping she might choose you. If you weren't prepared or didn't like your teacher, you sat there fidgeting, trying not to make eye contact. When you have been called, you are chosen and responsible to respond.   In this book you will find a great calling, my prayer is that you would respond as Isaiah by declaring, "here I am, send me!"

Being called isn't an oppressive or controlling thing. Instead, it denotes a choice and represents a people with freedom. Being called out identifies you as a person able to make a decision, a people that is alive and moving. Church is not a static address, Church is a movement. To call out a cement building seems kind of silly, unless we are talking about calling the people who are inside it to the outside and beyond!

The call is simple, and the movement's direction plain. We are aimed at Jesus, and to recognize Him in the face of the poor. We are called out of our routines and programs into relationships and love. Moving from the four walls of denomenational church, God is calling us into the workplaces and homes of our everyday lives. We are called out of our boxes of comfort to bring revival to a broken world. Can you hear the call?

God can use anyone that is willing. I have seen a 20 year old girl from Ohio run a successful orphanage in El Salvador, a NFL football player take in recovering addicts into his home, and a hollywood producer walk the city's at-risk kids down the red carpet and have the celebrities on the side asking for autographs. There are stay at home moms who have started apostolic prayer meetings for San Diego pastors and homeless hippies have multiplied bread and peanut butter to feed the multitudes on the streets. We are all created with destiny and are capable of doing far more than most people would ever aprove of. Almost everyone in history that I have ever studied that did something great for Jesus suffered persecutions from the "church". I don't care if you have a degree or not. It is not my concern if you have enough funding or a good business plan. Jesus can do more with less anyways. Our sole concern is to do the will of the Lord.

Jesus doesn't call the qualified, He qualifies the Called. No matter where you're from, or what earthly realities you believe you live in, Jesus is Calling You Out! There will never be the right time where it costs you nothing. There is only this moment, every moment, where we say "yes!" to Jesus no matter what the cost. It's time to walk in Heaven and cast out hell.

Ekklesia

"To the Church of God that is in Corinth, to those sanctified in Christ Jesus, called to be saints..."
~1 Corinthians 1:2a

One of the first Christian songs that I listened to is a Michael W. Smith song entitled "Finding My Place in this World." The song still sends chills running through my body as it resonates with my heart's deep desire to find that place where I belong. We were all created with a purpose and a destiny that would blow us away if we could only see it. I remember lying on my bed at night in my last year of high school with the song on repeat, allowing images of all my potential destinies and destinations to flood my nearly unconscious imagination until I fell asleep. This was my beginning in dreaming with God.

Where are you going? It seems we all long to be somewhere that we're not. People tend to see the grass as always greener. They run from place to place, go on vacation to different destinations, switch careers constantly, never settled or satisfied. All of us are in search of our own personal destiny. Whether it's tangible places, metaphysical ideals, or a different crowd of people, we want to find our perfect fit... the place where we are most fully alive.

For those pursuing God revealed in the person of Jesus Christ, the place they often go to find this is "church." In its purest form, the act is intentioned as a move from wherever you find yourself towards God. It has not been too challenging for people to identify with what Blaise Pascal called, "man's inherent God shaped void." The problem is that there's a disconnect. People are not finding what they're looking for, and they still have their voids. People go to "church" looking for the God in whom there is the fullness of life and freedom, only to find the same unhappy and controlling people. Too many people are moving on, still longing and still looking.

I realize that before I continue I should define "church" so that I don't need to keep putting quotations around the word. When speaking of church, I will define the word in two ways. The first I will write with a capitol "C," Church. The Church is the legitimate body of

Christ. It is every person who is a child of God, and whose inheritance is the kingdom. It is this Church that is to be the bride of Christ. I would never badmouth Jesus' wife. I only have the deepest and most profound love for the Church.

The second understanding of church is spelled with a lower case "c," and operates on a significantly more modern precept. The local church that you attend on Sunday mornings would fall into this category, along with any denominations such as a Baptist church, Roman Catholic church, Lutheran church or Church of the Nazarene. This is the miracle happening anytime two or three gather in Jesus' name and when Christ becomes present among us. I want to express my opinion up front that the church is a good thing, as long as it understands what it is and how it operates within the larger Church of which Christ is the head.

There is a reformation needed in the church, one that moves beyond the walls of our establishments. We need to move from playing church to being the Church, a pure and spotless bride. This is where we, as followers of Jesus, truly become the body of Christ. Where Jesus comes and "abides in us as we abide in him" (John 15:4). To call a building with four walls the Church is actually not scriptural. Jesus is not going to marry a building. This is not some modern revelation, but rather goes back to Jesus and his apostles and the original definition of "Church."

In the Bible, every time the word Church appears in the Bible, the Greek word used is *ekklesia*. This word *ekklesia* appears 74 times in the New testament, and it is foundational for what it means to be a follower of Jesus. This word for Church literally means "Called Out." The roots of the word in the greek are *ek* and *kaleo*. The *ek* denotes origin and refers to the point of origin of which something moves out of or comes from.   It also   is speaking to the necessity to move from one place to another. *Kaleo* is to call or to beckon. For Jesus and in the scriptures, the Church is the one "Called Out."

Israel was God's chosen. God had marked them as His own. He was jealous for them, and showed them great favor. One of God's greatest moves of love towards Israel was calling them out of Egypt and leading them into the Promised Land. The calling was clear and beautiful, but they still had to respond, trusting in God's power to deliver them from Pharaoh. The land they were called to was filled with giants, and their journey began with many wanderings and wars. Many people ignorantly wanted to return to the slavery of Pharaoh and Egypt. However, God was always faithful. He supernaturally provided both food and clothing for them. He led them in a glory cloud during the day and gave them fire in the night. God's calling was not easy, but He made it possible. The reward was freedom.

The name Israel means "the powerful prince of God." *Isra* comes from Sara, which means powerful prince, and *el* being God. Israel was the object of God's affection, God's sons and daughters, whose inheritance is the Kingdom of Heaven. Eventually, Israel's hearts were hardened, and when Jesus came they rejected him. This is all a part of God's beautiful redemptive plan that allowed God to create a new Israel. God's great act of love was toward everyone, and the new Israel is those who respond to His call, Jew or not.

God has opened his invitation to the world. God "desires all people to be saved and to come to the knowledge of the truth" (1 Tim. 2:4). The offer to be delivered from the bondages of sin and to become God's free children has been extended to all people. God has declared that you are a chosen race, a royal priesthood, a holy nation, a people for his own possession, that you may proclaim the excellencies of Him who called you out of darkness and into His marvelous light(1 Peter 2:9). We need to trust and believe in God's power to deliver us from satan, and we need to believe that He will be able to part the Red Sea for us as well. We have a beautiful calling, a final destination of heavenly proportions.

Many Christians, myself included, are really good at noticing what people are doing wrong and telling them how not to do it. Don't do this, don't do that, don't go there! While these exhortations can be needed, what we are forgetting to do is to tell them where they should go! What it is you can be doing! We are quick to point out the darkness, but never get around to talking about what the "marvelous light" looks like. You probably have felt that way about me so far. Some of you are sitting there saying, "Ok Paul, I get it. I'm called out. But where is this place and what does it look like? What exactly is it that we are called to?"

No matter what, you are called to prosper. Our final destination is Heaven and we are called to be heavenly people, walking out heavenly realities now. We are invited to be seated in Heavenly places with Christ, bringing His Kingdom on earth at it is in Heaven. As heirs to the throne with Christ, we are invited into this path that Jesus longs to walk with us, moving from Glory to Glory. This is the Good news of the Kingdom!

Discipling Nations

"And when they saw him they worshiped him, but some doubted. And Jesus came and said to them, 'All authority in heaven and on earth has been given to me. Go therefore and make disciples of all nations, baptizing them in the name of the Father and of the Son and of the Holy Spirit, teaching them to observe all that I have commanded you. And behold, I am with you always, to the end of the age.'"
~Matthew 28:17-20

Some of the most powerful, plain and directive words that Jesus ever gave the Church were also his very last before He ascended to heaven. This scripture, Matthew 28:17-20, has been at the heart of many churches and mission organizations for centuries. Each line is packed with revelation and direction, but I find the first one exceptionally encouraging.

<u>Matt. 28:17</u> And when they saw him they worshiped him, but some doubted.

When we read what has been coined as "the great commission," it is easy to catch ourselves seeing the "super" apostles moving in power, carrying the gospel throughout the world, but never believing in it for ourselves. However, this great calling was given to everyone, including the broken and those still struggling to find faith. It was among those who worshiped Jesus, even amidst their apparent doubts, that God's glory was made known. God isn't waiting until you get everything figured out, He wants to use you now.

"And Jesus came and said to them, "All authority in heaven and on earth has been given to me'" (Matt. 28:18).

Following the acknowledgement of the unqualified nature of His audience, Jesus reminds us of His power. When we feel weak, His strength is made manifest. We are like Peter and John, uneducated and common, but we are with Jesus. It is not about who we are, it's about who we're with. Jesus is the King of Kings and the Lord of Lords, supreme authority in all realities, both spiritual and physical. Jesus has been given the keys to death and Hades and has given them to His Church with a promise, "The gates of Hell will not prevail against it!" (Matt. 16:18b) The funny thing is a lot of people seem to think of this simply as an assurance that Hell won't come busting into the Church. I don't know when the last time you saw gates put on legs and come running after you, but I find it much more likely that this is an invitation. Keys open gates, and I think Jesus is inviting us into the domain of darkness to set the captives free.

Go therefore and make disciples of all nations, baptizing them in the name of the Father and of the Son and of the Holy Spirit" (Matt. 28:19).

This is the great calling to the believer. It starts with Go! God is not the God of no, He is the God of go! The gospel must be preached to all the corners of earth, bringing together the fullness of Christ's bride. The calling is not to go make converts. The calling isn't to go build churches. The calling is to go make disciples. Luke 14:33 says that if "any one of you does not renounce all that he has, he cannot be my disciple." This is not just a seminar. This is not just a Bible study. This is a leave-everything-and-follow-me Christ call. This is a call to make deep, transformational and powerful relationships. Let me share an example.

There are two brothers who have taught me more than maybe anyone else what it is to be a disciple. These brothers, Bryan and Brett, were 19 and 20 when they received the call of God. They were called out of their comfortable lives. They dropped out of college, in the face of their fears and the concerns of this world, and headed to the mission field. They moved in with me to a small, one-bedroom house with one goal: to live the authentic Gospel. We began to throw feasts for the homeless and take them into our house. Before we knew it there was no more room, not even floor space. As Bryan and Brett slept side by side with heroin dealers, murderers, and ex-convicts, they slept next to Jesus. They shared blankets and pillows with people who had AIDs, MRSA, staph infections and scabies. We were so poor that the homeless many times fed us. Through the lives of these young men, unknown to the world, hundreds of people's lives were radically impacted.

Wiccans repented, shamans traded crystals for crosses, heroin and meth were overcome with the love of Jesus, and even people with AIDs were healed. These two disciples are some of my heroes. They had no education, no supernatural visitation and no special skills (well, I guess Bryan is pretty good at the guitar). They made a decision to abandon all to become disciples and make disciples. They are just some of the few that receive the call of the gospel to a radically laid down life of love.

"...teaching them to observe all that I have commanded you. " (Matt. 28:20)

We cannot simply have lip service converts. We must love God, and Jesus said "if you love me you will keep my commands"(john 14:15). We must carry the Gospel to the broken and the poor all around the world, leading them in radical obedience. We need a people that will follow the Lamb wherever He leads. The call may seem a little radical. That's because it is. Impossible? Yes. But what is impossible for man is possible with God. The good news is that it is not obeying His commands that makes us lovers, but it is His love in us that compels us to live holy. This is why the call is followed with a promise of His presence.

In my last year of college, I received some incredibly important words of knowledge from internationally respected leaders. One of these words had to do with this great commission. This prophet told me he believed God was going to use me in creating a student- led missions movement, like the one Lou Engle had been foretelling. The weight of this word hit me with real sobriety. I wrestled with this calling, and it caused me no small worry. One night later that week I was tossing and turning in my bed unable to sleep, and in the middle of the night I went over to a spiritual father and woke him up. I told him with tears in my eyes, "the word you gave me scares me, and the calling is so big I don't know how I would ever go about doing it." He replied, "It won't happen because of your efforts, it will happen because it is God's desire, and it will flow out of who He is in you." This brought me comfort. I went to sleep and went on with life. Within a week of this night, one of the boys who I had been discipling received a dream from the Lord which told him that he was called to Cuenca, Ecuador. This friend was just one semester away from graduating, but he left everything and flew to Ecuador. Within the next six months, three more of those in my inner circle dropped out of school and left to the mission field. Never once did I ask them to do this. It is the Lord alone who calls us out, we just respond, "here I am, send me."

And behold, I am with you always, to the end of the age.'"

The great commission is placed between two promises. One is the promise of His presence and the other of His power. Jesus starts by saying He has all authority, and brings it home by saying "I am with with you." In order to walk out the radical lives God is calling us to, we need to be a people walking in awareness of His presence and His authority. Without His miraculous power and presence, we would have literally died. That power is easy to see when I have had MRSA outbreak and my skin is rotting off and I need Jesus to heal me, or when there is a Satanist lunging at me with his knife, but the reality is that it's true for all of us. If God withdrew His breath from any one of us, we would all die. The call just brings into light the already existent reality that we are all in desperate need of Jesus.

Clothed with Power

"Miracles are not contrary to nature, but only contrary to what we know about nature." ~**St. Augustine**

"And he said to them, "Go into all the world and proclaim the gospel to the whole creation. Whoever believes and is baptized will be saved, but whoever does not believe will be condemned. And these signs will accompany those who believe: in my name they will cast out demons; they will speak in new tongues; they will pick up serpents with their hands; and if they drink any deadly poison, it will not hurt them; they will lay their hands on the sick, and they will recover."

So then the Lord Jesus, after he had spoken to them, was taken up into heaven and sat down at the right hand of God.
And they went out and preached everywhere, while the Lord worked with them and confirmed the message by accompanying signs."
Mark 16:15-20

We are called to preach the Gospel. The Gospel is the "good news" that there is power for salvation. God is mighty to save from even the worst of circumstances. God can save your family. God can save this country. God can raise the dead, and we are to be about our Father's business.

The second account of the great commission is much more detailed and revealing. This is probably why it is such a hot topic for scholars. It reveals the gospel was never intended just to be a matter of talk, but involves power. When Jesus called people to come and follow Him, it involved doing the things that He did. Jesus said: *"Truly, truly, I say to you, whoever believes in me will also do the works that I do; and greater works than these will he do, because I am going to the*

Father" (John 14:12). The question we must ask ourselves is: do we believe in God and His Word?

We are not alone in ministry as the Church, but we are accompanied by the power of God, moving in the presence and gifts of the Holy Spirit. It says these signs will accompany those who believe (John 14:12, Mark 16:17). Jesus said if we had a mustard seed of faith, we could move a mountain. I see some mountains in society and in the church that could use some shaking. It's time to stir up some faith! I want to believe with the Church in a God that is alive and powerfully at work today in the lives of His followers, and who does what He says He does. Instead of thinking about the entertainment methods we can use to draw people in, how about we just start walking in our authentic destiny in the Lord? No one is sitting around bored when God shows up.

THEY WILL HEAL

"Is anyone among you sick? Let him call for the elders of the church, and let them pray over him, anointing him with oil in the name of the Lord.And the prayer of faith will save the one who is sick, and the Lord will raise him up. And

*if he has committed sins, he will be forgiven.
Therefore, confess your sins to one another and
pray for one another, that you may be healed.
The prayer of a righteous person has great
power as it is working."*
James 5:14-16

Many will contend that this promise is just for the
ancient apostles, but that is a obvious lie that the devil has
been able to weaken the church with. The gifts of the
Holy Spirit of our Lord Jesus Christ are available to all of
His Body, rationed out as He sees fit. Here in James 5 we
see an example of elders in the Church being specifically
commissioned to pray for healing in expectancy. No one
said the elders had "the gift of healing"! We all have
access to God, and we can ask for anything in the name
of the Father. Even the Old Testament shepherds were
expected to heal, as we see in Ezekiel 34 where they are
being rebuked for neglecting their job. *"The weak you
have not strengthened, the sick you have not healed, the
injured you have not bound up!"*

There are a number of great books out about the gift
of healing and its functions, and one of them is called 1
Corinthians. I am going to take this opportunity to share
with you some personal experiences of what this looks

like in our world today, and the ability it has to aid the great commission.

While visiting Iris Ministries in Mozambique, Africa, a small group of young adults went into the town hospital to carry out this healing commission. When we arrived, we proceeded to go with our interpreter into the infant wing of the hospital. Each wing of the hospital was a separate tent that held up to around 20 beds. Our team quickly set in praying for some of the children, but I felt the Lord was leading me elsewhere. I went into the tent I felt called to, but it was the adult intensive care branch and they all seemed to be Muslim. I was quickly kicked out as soon as I said the name "Jesus." I went into the street and asked if anyone needing healing. Those who responded were healed, including one man with a portable IV. I was able to get back into the tent that had kicked me out with a small team and finally convinced a guy to let us pray for him. He sat up in his bed and said he was totally healed.

We proceeded to move throughout the tent, praying for the Muslim men who had kicked me out just a few minutes before. The second guy we prayed for got out of his bed, -an IV still budding out of his foot- and walked around praying with us in the name of Jesus. This man had been Muslim. The healings were all taking place in plain view of the other patients, and there was an incredible momentum of faith growing. We walked up to a man in a coma and commanded that he come out. He responded and was able to hear the Gospel, maybe in the last few days of his life! A fully paraplegic man moved all his arms and legs, rolling over to yell at us for healing him in the name of Jesus since he was Muslim! The miracles happening were so radical, that I was challenged to even believe I was seeing correctly. The group even testified that I had wiped off a third degree burn with my hand, revealing new skin. If it was not for the group of people following me, and the articles written about it. I might not even have the faith to share the experience. What's amazing is that the extent of my vocabulary in Portuguese was "Can I pray for you? Are you sick? Be healed in the name of Jesus! Get up! Walk! Praise Jesus! Thank you Jesus!"

The kingdom of God is not a matter of talk, it is a matter of power! I was not saying any special magic words, I was not convincing the Muslims with my smart words, I was letting Jesus show Himself strong! The power of God to heal was transforming lives! Every person we prayed for in that wing of the hospital professed to be healed or showed visable signs of recovery, all of whom had previously been in critical condition and on IV's. Trust me, evangelism is a lot easier when people are climbing out of hospital beds.

When the miraculous is foreign to us, it is easy to think that it would only happen in foreign countries. But this is not true. Let me share an example of a group of friends going out for a good time with me in San Diego while at college:

It was a Friday night in late October 2008. A group of us decided to go out next to the bars in Ocean Beach and share the Gospel. The Lord led us into a dark alleyway behind some clubs and bars. We didn't see anyone so most people left, but I stayed with a couple others and waited to see what God wanted to do. After a few minutes, a girl in her twenties hobbled out the back door of one of the clubs into the alley. She was alone, drunk and had a broken ankle.

I asked her if we could pray for her, and she declined. I asked if there was anything in the world that she wanted, and she belligerently said that she would take a nice big bag of marijuana. I told her I didn't have that, but that we would pray and she could be healed of her broken ankle. She asked if we were magic people. We laughed and shared with her the Good News, and how that by Jesus' stripes we are healed. She shrugged and said, "sure, what the hell." We prayed and she felt waves of heat going through her leg up into her body. She was instantly and totally healed. Not only that, she became completely sober and spent the rest of the night going around to the bars she had just been in sharing how Jesus was real, and how He had healed and saved her. This was just one of many miracles we saw this night.

THEY WILL CAST OUT DEMONS

Have you ever tried to preach the gospel to someone and they just seemed hostile? It can be incredibly challenging when you are trying to convince a demon that Jesus is Lord. Few people have a problem believing that angels are real. It is even commonly understood that we have guardian angels (at least one for every person). The Bible tells us that one- third of the angels fell, and are now demons (Rev. 12:4). There are more than we think.

I could recall countless times where I have been preaching the good news of salvation to someone with little-to-no progress. After realizing there was a demonic presence, I addressed their oppression first and then was able to bring the person to know Jesus. Here is one such story:

I have a friend who lives on the streets that everyone calls "Firewalker." Firewalker has spent his life on the streets. His dad lives on the streets and for decades they have both been struggling with alcohol and drugs. Firewalker earned his name because of occult practices involving holding fire and walking through fire. The heavy toll of drugs and the occult caused Firewalker to wander aimlessly around the bonfire pits of OB. Whenever our outreach teams would talk to him, he would always ramble on about how he was an "ancient one" and talk about his reincarnation. He stumbled everywhere and always encouraged people to "stumble well." The gospel was preached to him many times, falling on deaf ears.

During one Friday night outreach, I was walking a girl to the bathroom (our outreaches are often intense so we don't let girls walk alone). Along the way she got pulled aside, was pushed into the sand, and Firewalker attempted to rape this young girl half his age. This ended my nice tactics with Firewalker. I pulled Firewalker off of her, grabbed him in my hands and began to speak in tongues, commanding the demons to leave. Firewalker began to forcibly shove sand down his throat, and his demons tried to kill him on their way out. I commanded them to stop and prayed for few minutes, after which

Firewalker's demons finally left. Firewalker repented, cried for over an hour and prayed to receive the Holy Spirit.

At our next Friday outreach, Firewalker cooked everyone dinner with the little he saved up from panhandling during the week. He quickly became our outreach "bonfire tender," (he did have some serious ability with fire afterall), and came faithfully week after week. Firewalker has his ups and downs, and is just at the beginning of this journey. But he reads the Bible, has a tender heart, and will always say he is thankful for "the day he got set free!"

No amount of convincing could ever have persuaded Firewalker. You cannot argue with demons, they are liars and are unaccountable. It is going to be an uphill battle attempting to bring the good news to a broken world if you don't believe that Jesus offers freedom from bondage. However, we must remember to love people! We cannot find ourselves on a witch-hunt. I want to join Jesus in destroying the works of the devil, without destroying people.

One time I was in a remote African village that had some of the heaviest witchcraft I had ever seen. There was literally a witch dressed all in red who was floating around in the meeting. When I saw her staring at me, peering up at me through her stringy, black hair, I immediately was cursed and became sick in front of a bunch of my friends. I had my friend Nathan pray to break its power and I was healed instantly. We cannot do everything alone, and often it takes someone else to break the chains over our life.

The next day I met a young boy, probably about three years old. It was obvious that he was the reject of the village. His bloodshot eyes had flies stuck to them, his belly was bloated, and his hands and feet were cracked. A mixture of mud and blood was plastered over his whole body. This boy had probably been raped, because he would make sexual gestures at you and try to grope you. The boys of the village would try to throw him away from you, because they knew he was blatantly trying to steal from you. I was convinced this boy had been cursed by the witch, and I knew he was fully possessed. I also knew he had to get free.

Because I had a heart for the child, I shooed all of the village boys away and tried to pray deliverance over him. I tried to pray as he clambered over me, grabbing at me, continually trying to steal from me. I tried to hold him while I commanded his demon to leave. Yet I was mostly getting beat, scratched, and bitten. I began to learn that people have free will and can freely choose bondage. You cannot force someone into freedom, or else they wouldn't be free.

As I was lying in the dirt, basically wrestling with this three year old boy, a young girl from our team came over. Taking her bottle of water, and using the hem of her long dress, she began to wash the boy's feet. As the bloody dirt collected on her shirt, the boy and I both broke in tears. This simple act of love sent the demons fleeing, as "perfect love casts out fear." The boy wasn't able to receive my exorcism, but he was able to receive an act of sacrificial love. Love is always enough.

THEY WILL SPEAK IN NEW TONGUES

Shrouded in mystery, the gifts are supernatural in nature and are always an offense to the natural mind, as is stated in Paul's address to the Corinthians in chapter 14. I want to point out that Paul wishes we would all speak in tongues, and also claimed to speak in tongues more than all of us. Jesus said those who believe would speak in new tongues, and Paul exhorts us not to forbid speaking in tongues, but rather to pursue the spiritual gifts.

The gift of tongues seems to be multi-faceted. There are tongues of men and tongues of angels. There are tongues for the believer and tongues as a sign to the unbeliever. There are depths to speaking in tongues that go beyond the rational mind and that delve deep into places of spiritual worship and communion. It is a powerful tool to build oneself up, and to give high praise unto the Most High. I encourage everyone to pray through 1 Cor. 14 asking God for cognitive understanding into this gift, but even more I ask the Holy Spirit to activate it within you. We can often have the gifts, and just need to fan them into flame (2 Tim. 1:6). Just as we could have the gift of healing, and never reach out our hands and proclaim, "be healed," we could have the gift of tongues and never praise Jesus "in the Spirit." If you want to speak in tongues and you are filled with the spirit, why not ask Jesus and try.

Since so much can be said on the subject, I am just going to give you two examples. One that explains tongues *for* the believer, and one that shows them as a sign *to* the unbeliever.

Tongues edify those praying:

Romans 8:26 says that the Spirit makes intercession for us with groans too deep for words. When we are not experiencing breakthrough in our wordy prayers, it can be time to enter into intercession in the spirit. When our first house church was bursting at the seams, with people sitting on each others laps in our biggest room(the garage), we realized we needed a bigger meeting place. I had received a vision a couple years earlier where God showed me an upstair bar on a main strip with music floating out of the open windows. People were being drawn out of the other bars and were coming in and worshiping Jesus. About a month before our prayer meeting, I had seen this exact upstair bar in the middle of Newport St. in Ocean Beach and had been praying. I even even sent an email to their owner to no avail. With everyone crammed in our little garage, I asked everyone to cry out in the Spirit for this building. As everyone interceded in tongues, my phone began to ring. I stepped outside and picked up. On the phone was the owner of the Bar (who I had never met) and he told me he wanted to give me the bar on sundays for free. I have seen many walk up those stair uninvited, giving their lives to Jesus. Three people even gave their lives to Jesus outside the building and started praising him in the alley behind saying, "We feel the presence of Jesus in this music, we will turn our lives over to Him!" Eventually, after holding services there for over a year, the drug dealers and owners left the business in order to seek out a new and more fulfilling life. Sure this left us without a sunday building, but it also left Ocean Beach with one less drug dispensary and bar.

Tongues for the Unbeliever:
1Cor. 14:22 *Thus tongues are a sign not for believers but for unbelievers*

I will admit, I include this testimony primarily because I enjoy it so very much. The Holy Spirit can be so much fun, and wow does God have a sense of humor!

It was a beautifully warm summer night in California. A couple of friends of mine had been with me at a Holy Ghost house party. The Glory of God really came as these young adults took their friday night and turned their eyes toward Jesus in pure joyful devotion. Sometime around one in the morning we left to drive our musician friend home. Our friend was visiting and was staying out in the country outside town. On the drive out, my well known musician friend told me he was honestly a little offended by some of the manifestations of the Holy Spirit. At that point in my walk I honestly agreed. Together we prayed to Jesus that God would blow up our paradigms if it was Him.

Once we were well into the country, on a lonely country road, we were awestruck with the beauty of God's creation. The night was so lovely and the stars were shining as brightly as any of us could recall seeing. We pulled over and decided to lie, all 5 of us, on top of my car roof to watch the stars (needless to say the dents are still there). After some time of sweet fellowship, a random car pulled over right in front of us. The driver got out and approached us and we all got down to go meet him. The driver was a rowdy guy in his mid 20's, metalica shirt on, obviously on his way home from a party. The stranger asked us if we were lost. I told him no and asked if he was lost. He said no. I proclaimed "Great! Then you know Jesus!" At this he replied, "No, I don't know Jesus." I asked plainly, "Would you like to?" He said yes. My dear well intentioned friend began to lead this man in the classic religious "repeat after me for Jesus to come into my life" prayer. I got on my knees as I watched this new man get introduced to religion, untouched. I felt something welling up inside of me and a cry came from my inmost being. I cried out loud, "Holy

Spirit Come!". The Holy Spirit dropped like a bomb and all of my friends who had gathered around this man fell out onto the cement. My friend who had said he wasn't sure what to think about all the manifestations flew back so hard, he rolled off to the side of the road laughing hysterically. The random stranger just stood looking at all of us confused. I was lying on the ground laughing as Jesus told me to pick him up and spin him over my shoulder. I leaned over and asked one of my friends who was lying on the ground near me if that was a good idea. They replied, "Paul, you will not do that. I repeat. No." But the Holy Spirit persisted as this man stood there, unencountered. I got up. Ran up to the man and threw him over my shoulder like a fireman. I spun him around three times and then placed him on his feet. As soon as I put him down the Holy Spirit fell on him and he was baptized in the Holy Spirit. He fell to the ground shouting in tongues and laughing.

The gift of tongues was a sign to him that this was real and that there really was a Holy Spirit. I have seen similar things happen with others in our ministry. I have prayed for homeless who have fallen out speaking in tongues. This is always a sign to them of the presence and power of the Holy Spirit. They still need to make a decision to follow Jesus, but it is a powerful encounter that certainly points to the existence of an all powerful God.

THEY WILL BE PROTECTED

<u>Psa. 91:14</u>   *"Because he holds fast to me in love, I will deliver him;I will **protect** him, because he knows my name.*

Make no mistake, I believe in Martyrdom. I embrace the fact that a loving God allows His saints to suffer and even die for him, and see this as the greatest crown to a believer's life. The bible tells us that blessed are we when we suffer trials of many kinds.   Held in tension with this reality, is that we have a God who is might to save!

Throughout history there have been countless stories of the miraculous protection of God for his saints. One of the first Christian martyrs named Polycarp was recorded to be unburnable at the stake. Present day Brother Yun is another example, who was in prison for the gospel and had his legs miraculously restored after being shattered by the guards. He then proceeded to walk out of the open high security prison gates unnoticed. The bible tells us that it is not His will that any one should perish. The devil comes to steal, kill, and destroy. Jesus came to destroy the works of the devil.

Wether it is simply in the dark alleys of San Diego or wether I am hitchhiking my way through South Africa, the Lord has protected me. One story that me and my wife Katie think is fun happened as we ventured into Mexico for the first time after we got engaged. Our ministry in San Diego takes trips into our Mexico base at least once a month, and I personally go more frequently. I am very comfortable in Mexico and both Katie and I have a deep love for the country. This being said, Mexico can be really sketchy. On our drive home from Ensenada it began to pour down in torrents of rain. A couple hours later we came down between the mountain pass into Tijuana. As we began to drive up the shallow grade, the street began to flood. The road quickly was transformed into a river right before our eyes, as the waters rose higher and higher, trapped in on both sides. Our car began to float backwards as our wheels lifted off the pavement. The water level was up to our windows and the inside was flooding. As our car filled up with water, our tires remained mostly on the ground. The water rose up to the top of our seats, Katie standing on her seat, my foot still on the gas pedal, completely submerged. My car at the time was a silver 2004 Toyota Matrix. I don't have any special off-road package or snorkel. My intake was completely underwater as we continued to slowly drive forward, mostly uphill, for the next 20 minutes. When we finally got out of the pass to a turnout, we drove uphill onto dry ground. We opened my doors and the water poured out of all sides. Katie, Me, and my car were completely unharmed, other than smelling like Tijuana sewer for a month.

True Religion

*Religion that is pure and undefiled before God,
the Father, is this:
to visit orphans and widows in their affliction,
and to keep oneself unstained from the world*
~ James 1:27

In recent years the term religion has taken quite a
beating. Slogans like "I'm not religious" or "it's not
religion, it's a relationship," can be heard shouted from
the lips and literature of many of the churches and
believers around the world. I frequently hear
charismatics renounce the "religious spirit." Though we
may be identifying a real problem, the problem is not
religion, it is our definition and expression of religion.
The bible does not condemn religion, it demands a radical
redefinition of religion.

True Religion is not just a designer pair of jeans, it is giving up those jeans for someone who has less. The Kingdom of God is for the poor, and Jesus said that He came for the sick, not the well. The religion that God is pleased with is not in our large fellowships, but rather our fellowship with the least of these. Religion is not stain glass windows, it is remaining unstained from the lusts of this world.

There is a lot of hurt in the body of Christ by "religion" and by "the church" that can create bitterness, resentment and isolation. I propose that they have identified an impostor! The devil has crept in among the churches and disillusioned many to believe they were being "sheep bitten." News Flash: sheep don't bite, wolves in sheep's clothing do. This may be offensiv,e but the bible says that we will "know them by their love for one another." If we begin to identify the enemy as satan, and begin to hate what he has done and is doing in our churches, then we can begin to love the Church again.

Allow me to use a metaphor to expose the devil's agenda to defile the bride. My wife's name is Katie. When I hear the name Katie, what I think of is a beautiful and wonderful blessing from Jesus. However, if people on the street started a new slang word and called prostitutes "Katies," it could be hurtful and defiling. Now when I talk about "my Katie" people think of a prostitute. They may begin to think things of me and my wife that are not true. Katie is not a prostitute. She is a lovely woman who is pure and undefiled. The Church is not a prostitute. The Church is the beautiful bride of Christ. Allow me tell you about this beautiful bride.

The Church is wonderfully religious. The body of believers that Jesus is going to marry is full of love and light. Religion is the garments of purity and compassion for the poor, the fine white linens the Bride wears down the aisles of Heaven. We are the people who stop for the one on the side of the road and are not afraid of their smell, but are in love with their hearts. The Church is made up of all those beautiful hearts that have gone out to the nations, giving up their lives in love for people groups they have never known. It is the nameless saint ministering to God in a back pew, and the zealous street evangelist whose heart is breaking for the lost. It is the religious Church that clothes the naked, feeds the hungry and brings the homeless poor into their house. True religion is at the heart of "Social Justice" and has an even more radical expression of Social Mercy.

Amidst meeting the needs of the world, the Church is so much more than a great humanitarian aide.

When I hear James 1:27 quoted, it is usually stated only in part. It is not only care for the poor, it is also walking in purity. It is great when a movement understands God's heart for the widows and the orphans and dives deep into the depths of the darkness of the world. This is absolutely God's heart. It is beautiful and much needed. Meanwhile, we need to be "in the world, and not of the world." It is not enough to just be in the world. We cannot conform in an effort to save. Whenever we let our love for people triumph over our love for God, we have lost the ability to do both. The truest form of love rests wholly in the One who IS love. If we conform to the world and lose our identity in Christ as a people of the light, then we have nothing to offer the world anyways. This broken world needs much more than another social justice cause, we need a Savior. If we feed their bodies just to watch their spirits starve, we eternally fail them.

The Church meets both the physical and spiritual needs of this world and it is through the all encompassing means of Jesus. The man who could turn a little boy's lunch into a feast for thousands really can be the answer for desperate multitudes. As the Church we may feel like we could never actually multiply food for the thousands, which I would disagree with, but at a minimum you could at least be the boy who sacrifices his lunch. Remember, whatever you do to the least of these in Jesus' name you do to him. We cannot run around claiming the name of Jesus if we have no heart for the very people he died for. We must serve in the name of Jesus. There is only one way and one name under heaven by which we are saved. It is true that if you skip the name and just do the works that you will avoid sure persecution. I am sure you will get turned away less often and people's demons will not manifest, as they will not be threatened. Without the name of Jesus we lose everything. In the name of Jesus there is salvation.

A Wedding Story

"Wives, submit to your own husbands, as to the Lord.
For the husband is the head of the wife even as Christ is
the head of the church, his body, and is himself its Savior.
Now as the church submits to Christ, so also wives should
submit in everything to their husbands. Husbands, love
your wives, as Christ loved the church and gave himself
up for her, that he might sanctify her, having cleansed
her by the washing of water with the word, so that he
might present the church to himself in splendor, without
spot or wrinkle or any such thing, that she might be holy
and without blemish. In the same way husbands should
love their wives as their own bodies. He who loves his
wife loves himself. For no one ever hated his own flesh,
but nourishes and cherishes it, just as Christ does the
church, because we are members of his body. "Therefore
a man shall leave his father and mother and hold fast to
*his wife, and the two shall become one flesh." **This***
mystery is profound, and I am saying that it refers to
Christ and the church.
~ Ephesians 5:22-32

Imagine with me a wedding, maybe your wedding. Try to see things from the groom's perspective, peer down the aisle and see your bride walking toward you. She has been waiting for this moment all of her life. She looks beautiful in a glowing white dress as her eyes stare intently into yours. Your heart is pounding in your chest. But all of a sudden her left leg starts to drag and can't seem to catch up with the right, so she just tries to drag it along. Her right hand starts to spasm, and she accidentally smacks one of the onlookers in an aisle seat. All the parts of her body seam to have been individually possessed with their own agenda. The left arm, the only sane part of her body left, tears itself from her and tries to run, only to end up flopping helplessly on the floor. The Bridegroom falls onto his knees, weeping bitterly for his bride who is self destructing before his eyes. The audience has a plethora of reactions from shame to shock, bitterness, outright anger, confusion - the whole spectrum of concerned and hurt emotions. That Bride is the Church and the Groom is Christ, and the whole world has been watching us trying to get down the aisle.

Sure, there may have been good intentions. The left leg may have just remembered that she had left something in the dressing room, the right arm probably had no good excuse, and the left arm just saw everything else that was happening and, understandably, didn't want to be a part of it. The problem is no different than in most of our marriages and can be boiled down to communication. The body of Christ has not been able to communicate with one another. The right leg needs to walk in step with the left leg, not necessarily moving in the same way at the same time, but in tandem under the direction of the head. There needs to be steady leadership. Jesus is our only hope, no other leadership will do.

The problem may seem simple, but its solution may not be quite so easy. The church might be quick to respond, saying "how fortunate we are, that *We* may provide a stable head for the Body." The problem is that the church is just an arm or a leg of a Body that only Jesus Christ can be the head of. Christ has one direction, one agenda, and one theology. We should be the most united people on the face of the planet. Seeing as how the world religions and humanists have whole libraries of books, and we get to rally around one!

Ok, I can already hear the responses. I acknowledge there are different interpretations of the Bible, the living word of God. It is not hard to see the different agendas of the church down the street. Part of this variation is healthy, for if the body were made up of all hands, we would never get anywhere. We need missionary focused churches, we need politically active churches, we need the houses of prayer for all nations. Likewise, we need the Catholic reverence for scripture and God. We could all learn from the simplicity of the Amish and believe in an ever present and miraculous God like the Pentecostals. Wesley's understanding of God's power to annihilate sin is a beautiful revelation of God's power in a believer's life. The problem is when the hand tears itself from the body and refuses to participate actively in the body as a whole. We can see this frequently when denominations only go to *their* camps, read *their* theology, support *their* missionaries, etc. We too often fail to recognize the reconciling nature of the message of Jesus. We must resist the temptation to feel threatened by those who are different than us. We are in need of a liberation from our theological prejudices. Somehow we need to find a way to believe that Jesus had a theology bigger than our boxes, one that his whole Body fits in, one where all his attributes are embraced.

Now I must admit that it will be a constant struggle for me not to contribute to the problem even in writing this. The fleshly desire of an insecure man is to criticize, or to have all the answers. It is this very critical nature that has propagated such a significant problem as we face today. Jesus said, "blessed is He who is not offended with me." It would do us well to remember what was said to Paul on the road to Damascus, "stop persecuting *me*!" When we are offended with the Bride and respond in persecution, we are doing it onto Jesus.

I do not have all the answers, nor do I have all the "right" theology. Hopefully you don't find any heresies in me, or add me to the growing 25 million that have been martyred for there "heresies." We see only in part and I pray that we can engage each other in such boldness of truth... in the humility of our present human state. We need to be able to dialogue again so that we can work as a coherent whole. The church is in need of a reformation towards reconciliation, without making that statement an oxymoron. Indeed, Reformation is a necessity. I believe we can safely agree that a response to the practices of indulgences, a practice where essentially salvation can be bought at a monetary value, was a valid motivation for one of the most significant early reformations. There have been a number of reformations that have been made in legitimate efforts to maintain the integrity of the

Gospel. I find this issue pressing in light of Jesus' statement that "Every kingdom divided against itself is laid waste, and no city or house divided against itself will stand" (Matt. 12:25).

I believe that this movement towards unity is going to have to come on many fronts. Actually, on every front. I believe that the individual wills of the various parts of the Body of Christ, ie. Catholic, Wesleyan, Pentecostal, Lutheran, Reformed, Eastern, etc., are going to need to move back into coherency as a whole. We must not think we can come along from the outside and push everyone together, or be a hand forcing the legs to move "rightly" in tandem. Rather we must all come intentionally back to the call of the Head, specifically the instruction of Jesus towards one mind in Him. Let the call be heard for a grass roots movement towards a love of our brothers in Christ. Matthew, Mark, Luke, John, Paul, etc. all had different views of who Jesus is, and they all had different theological agendas. However, what's important is that they all fit into the paradigm of the Love of a Savior for a broken world, found in a God come as man, our Lord Jesus Christ.

Jesus was simple. Sure He was a transcendent fully God, fully man, king savior guy, but he liked to keep it simple. If someone was hungry, we ought to feed them. If someone was injured, well shoot, God could heal him (and even "willed" to 100% of the time!). But Jesus! What about this? Jesus how about that? It seems the questions fill the Gospels. And Jesus could so cooly reply, Love. Jesus reminds us that "we need to become like children to see the Kingdom," we must return to the simpler way.

I personally have a lot of pretty good theological questions for probably all major religious institutions. I even have some pretty clever answers. But it becomes a little concerning that Jesus didn't seem to value theology quite like we do. He made it very clear that we are not His "brother" just because we understand God well. After all, satan probably understands the Trinity better than I. Rather, because we love God in doing His will, we are valued as co-heirs. The will of the Father is to Love, and let us be reminded by Theresa of Avila that, "if we keep judging people, we will have no time to love them."

The Church needs to move from a spirit of criticism and division, to the Spirit of grace, unity and love; the Spirit of Jesus. For many of the churches, we can see the various sins in the sand as our own theological faults. When Jesus does not cast stones at the prostitute for her misbehavior, who are we to cast stones for misunderstanding. Sure, we may have some prostitutes in our theological midst, but many will fall within all of the various church doctrines and deserve correction, (dialogue) not condemnation.

Marriage is a constant metaphor in the Bible for the Church. Jesus is coming for a Bride, not a harem. Christ is going to continue to wash His Bride spotless and pure with the washing of His Word, and we should help him. I am all for Christian accountability and washing with the word in exhortation, correction, etc. We just need to be driving towards a unity in the authentic Gospel, and not dividing over the smaller issues. Don't leave your body and your head behind. It will only leave you alone, flopping stagnant and bloody.

Reformation of Reconciliation

"I do not ask for these only, but also for those who will believe in me through their word, that they may all be one, just as you, Father, are in me, and I in you, that they also may be in us, so that the world may believe that you have sent me. The glory that you have given me I have given to them, that they may be one even as we are one, I in them and you in me, that they may become perfectly one, so that the world may know that you sent me and loved them even as you loved me."
~ John 17:20-23

We must understand God's heart for unity. It was Jesus' final prayer that the Church would be unified in Him. The reasons to divide are too small in comparison with the desire of our Master! I recognize that not everyone who uses the name "Jesus" is talking about the one true God, much less knows Him or loves Him. But a unity that comes at the cost of conformity is a sure recipe for tyranny and the occult. A unity that is blessed with heavenly diversity is the heart of God, this is the Bride that Jesus so passionately longs for.

We cannot create any more divisions based on doctrines, music, or anything else that complicates the simplicity of the Gospel. I do believe reformation to the churches is long needed, and probably a continual need unto the day of redemption. However, it is the labor of unity that will empower the Church to bring in the great harvest Jesus longs for. When godly honor, submission, and even a little epistemological humility triumph over our pride and judgement, maybe then we will be positioned to love Jesus' Church.

In my journey I have ministered in many different ways and places. I have served as a worship leader, youth leader, street evangelist, marketplace minister, and even "head pastor." Whether in a Baptist, Episcopal, Presbyterian, Assemblies of God, Four Square, Nazarene, or non denomination church, I have been there. I cherish the inheritance of my Catholic Grandma who walked in love with the Lord when none of my family was living saved. Privileged, I stood along side Catholics praying for the end of abortion. I have served alongside Baptists who have spent their lives ministering in the garbage dumps of Tijuana. I have seen the power of the Gospel amongst the Pentecostals and Charismatics. First hand, I report that they all are loved by our King, and that many of them are radically in love with both Jesus and His people.

I have been asked to leave the Episcopal church unless I changed my views on abortion and homosexuality to adhere to a more "liberal" christian audience. I'm aware of the idolatry and witchcraft in the catholic church all around the world. I was told by the Presbyterian board that it was great that I had a heart to reach out to the poor, but just not to bring them back to church with me. I have fought through Nazarene board meetings because they wished to pass a grant for tens of thousands of dollars to build a wall to keep the homeless from sleeping on their property, while 5,000 dollar youth budget was being cut. This last one personally touched me so much that I broke down crying in the middle of the pastors meeting and cried out in prayer, "God shake their hearts and begin with the very foundations!" Immediately the room began to shake and a picture frame came crashing down off the wall! Needless to say, they repented of their bill, but I was let go for unclear reasons shortly thereafter. I do not share these experiences out of bitterness. I love what God is doing through all of these churches. I forgive them and bless them. Even more, I know the magnitude of His plans for these churches and want to see them walk in the fullness of their destiny! I share these life experiences to say that I am not unaware of the immense need for reformation. I want to see a spotless and pure bride for Jesus. I just think that disunity is one big spot, and that everything else will begin to accelerate as we join together.

Proverbs 18 starts off saying, "Whoever isolates himself seeks his own desire; he breaks out against all sound judgement." We need to live in the safety of a multitude of counselors, and they can't all be a part of the same locality of the Body. We need each other with our various skills and insights. The Catholics could teach the non-denominationals a lot about reverence, angels, and the value of communion, while the non-denominational churches could aide in an understanding of the priesthood of all believers and the friendly reminder to have no graven images or idols. When one sheep goes astray, we run after them. When one log catches fire, we gather near them. For a log burning by itself, no matter how big or how bright, will always burn out before the bundle that sticks together in the fireplace.

We must not forget our fathers. We are called in Isaiah 58 to rebuild the ancient ruins, and raise up the foundations of many generations. They may look like ruins, but we do not abandon them and just move on or lay a different foundation. God did not just destroy you and this whole earth when we went astray. With His very own blood He labored for restoration and unity. Jesus is into making all things new, but He brings life into the once dead things. Praise God He doesn't abandon the unfinished work, but is faithful to complete what He starts. I think the Church needs to be about its Father's business.

What I find so compelling is that most of the major reformers never wanted to cause a church/Church split. Luther never wanted to leave the Catholic church, he just felt morally bound to speak the truth that he believed. Likewise, Calvin and John Wesley all clung to their roots. The causes were worthy and not intentioned for dissension. I am not saying that we all should just become whatever our fathers are and wrestle it out, but rather to grasp the heart of unity that Jesus and all His

Saints expressed. Just like Luther, we have a disease that is corrupting our church. And just like Luther's time, all the world can see it except for the church. I champion the need for reformation, while standing in careful awareness of God's love for His kids.

The definition of insanity is doing the same thing over and over, expecting different results. I don't want any more movements "outside" of the Church. We need to restore the Church by a sweeping movement from within the churches. How can we ask for a revival in the secular world if we cannot steward what we already have within our churches? We cannot even imagine what God could do through His Church if it would unify in the Presence and Power of His Promised Holy Spirit. No matter what it costs. No matter what it looks like.

It is not my intention to say we need to do away with all denominations. Jesus will do that regardless. I am not telling everyone to join the non-denominational denomination or return to their catholic predecessors. I am not saying I have the answer. I just know that Jesus' heart is for unity among His Bride. At the end He is returning for a Bride, not a Harem.

To restore us to the unity and maturity of the pure and spotless bride will require many things. At the center is surely the Love of God poured out through His Holy Spirit. We also know according to Ephesians that it will be through the washing of the water of the Word. However, we are given an explicit key in the scriptures what this will look like.

The Five Fold Ministry

"And he gave the apostles, the prophets, the evangelists, the shepherds and teachers, to equip the saints for the work of ministry, for building up the body of Christ, **until** *we all attain to the* **unity** *of the faith and of the knowledge of the Son of God, to mature manhood, to the measure of the stature of the fullness of Christ, so that we may no longer be children, tossed to and fro by the waves and carried about by every wind of doctrine, by human cunning, by craftiness in deceitful schemes. Rather, speaking the truth in love, we are to grow up in every way into him who is the head, into Christ, from whom the whole body, joined and held together by every joint with which it is equipped, when each part is working properly, makes the body grow so that it builds itself up in love."*

~Ephesians 4:11-16

God's design for the church is through these "ascension" gifts, or otherwise know as the "five-fold ministry." Now many people have wrestled theologically if prophets or apostles still exist. I think it is interesting that they never question if pastors or evangelists still exist, yet they are less biblically addressed than apostles and prophets(The word pastor only exists this one time in the whole new testament). I believe the Bible is very clear in the timeline for these gifts. They're for the Church *until* we reach the unity of faith and full stature of Christ. So why the great disappearing act? It reasons that since the Bible teaches that the foundation of the Church is to be built on apostles and prophets that all the devil has to do to create disunity and immaturity, even impotence in the Church, would be to remove these two key positions.

I have heard all kinds of reasons that these two positions no longer exist, but I would greatly challenge anyone to reason with the Bible to see if they hold water. If an Apostle must have seen the risen Lord, then how did the Apostle Paul end up writing so much of the New Testament. "Well, it was in a vision," one may say. Good thing in the last days the Spirit of Prophecy will fall on all flesh and we will all see in visions and dreams (Acts 2, Joel 2). There are two great end time witnesses that prophesy day and night (Revelation 11:6). There is so much scriptural evidence that apostles and prophets are still for today that I will just leave it up to the anointing to show you.

Just like everything else in this life's journey, the point is to be closer to Jesus. The gifts of the various ministries are always God giving away a piece of His heart and allowing us to fellowship with Him in one of His functions. Jesus is the Chief Apostle, the greatest Prophet, the Evangel (good news) of the Evangelists, the good Teacher and Shepherd. When we receive the greatest gift of all, which is the Holy Spirit, we are filled with God Himself. In this sense any person could reveal the various roles of God at any needed time. You see that the apostle Paul was also called a teacher and an evangelist. He also was prophetic enough to write scripture as the inspired "word of the Lord." In this sense ,God can use us all to evangelize a lost neighbor, pastor our family, teach a new convert, prophesy truth and life, and even apostolicly build the Kingdom.

We need to let people be released to be the powerful, world changing Christians that God created them to be. Whatever we honor in life we bring increase to. I like to joke that if I honor the stray kitty at my door with some milk, you bet I will see an increase in stray kitty's presence. God is challenging His church today to begin to give honor to His prophetic and apostolic heart, and the people that He has anointed to walk in these roles. While I believe any person can reveal the nature of Christ in any of these five-fold ways, God has ordained certain individuals to be particularly strong in one area. Operating officially in a position of the five fold ministry brings increased teaching and revelation to that area through the example of their lives and the extraordinary function of their gifting. Jesus even tells us that if we honor a prophet in the name of a prophet, we will reap a prophet's reward. Let us come to be more motivated by the glorious reward than of the name of "a prophet". Apostles bring the safety and accountability of a Father. They hold everything before the plumbline of the word and the wisdom of God. Prophets give us guidance not according to man's ways, but according to God's direction. Where there is no prophetic direction, people cast off restraint. Where prophets flourish, God's will is released and the people prosper.

One of the major keys in reflecting on church history is the Church's responsibility to heed prophetic guidance. If the Catholic Church had been able to exercise the humility required to see its own fallibility and respond to the prophetic challenges of the 95 thesis, we would likely be dealing with a much different church dynamic today. Christians who see the Bible differently than us cannot be viewed as a threat, but rather as a gift of potential accountability that should drive us deeper into Jesus for the truth. When we cling too heavily to the comfort of our traditions, it can be hard to receive authentic revelations that are different than our previous notions, even if they are rooted deeply in scripture. However, God gave us a diverse bride with many different expressions, to create a very beautiful wife.

God's Design

these I will bring to my holy mountain, and
make them joyful in my house of prayer; their
burnt offerings and their sacrifices will be
accepted on my altar; for my house shall be
called a house of prayer for all peoples." The
Lord GOD, who gathers the outcasts of Israel,
declares, "I will gather yet others to him besides
those already gathered."
~Isaiah 56:7-8

Though it is my intention to create some sort of
working definition to the Church and our expression of
the local churches, I do not mean say I have it all figured
out. I cannot write a ten step guide to church as it should
be. If God wanted to, He would have done that. But
what God wanted is more of an Organism than an
Organization. He wanted something alive and moving,
not stagnant or static. We need to seek Him for His plans

for our lives and our cities. In this life it seems all too often we would rather just have His 12 step program than actually have to know Him.

God's way of taking us into His ways is different than we may think. One night I was crying out for direction and to know what exactly it was that He wanted me to do. He told me that even if He showed me where to go and what to do, it wouldn't help. I would be inadequate and overwhelmed. I then got scriptural with God and told Him, "but the psalms say show me the way and I will walk in it." God's like, "oh yeah, that place in Psalm 86 where it is written "teach me your way, O Lord, that I may walk in truth; unite my heart to fear your name." Oh boy. It was about the heart the whole time. God doesn't show us something external and have us inwardly strive towards that thing. Rather, He gives us a piece of His heart, His values and DNA, and moves in us from the inside out. Who He is in us will necessarily manifest into the world around us.

An example of this theological truth in action can be seen in the ministry God has me in today. We have started many mission bases, recovery homes and house churches all over California and Mexico. If God had told me in my early years to start a recovery home I would have researched all the right models, I would have sought all the right council, made my three year plan and totally missed what God wanted to do with me. God didn't want another institutional program. He wanted a passionate people who would love the poor. So instead, God put His love for the poor in my heart. Necessarily, when I saw the street kids lying in the street when it began to rain, I took them into my house. Out of the overflow of my heart for them to prosper, we went deeper into discipleship and intentionality. The result was a love driven group of people who develop God centered family with the orphans of our society. This is something that is contagious and everyone can be a part of.

With the heart in mind, I do want to attempt to portray just a few of the principles Jesus gives us to work with. There are many amazing insights that scripture gives us and kingdom principles that we are to build with. While each person is unique and each mission field different, God is always the same. He is unchanging and unwavering in His love, and His values are across the board.

When Jesus walked into the "church" of the day it was not only to pat their backs and encourage them with positive words. It was one of the most interesting portraits of Jesus in all of scripture, where He drives people out with a whip and calls it a den of thieves.

After flipping over the tables in His all consuming zeal for "His Father's House," He directs us that it is to be a "House of Prayer" that is "For All Nations."

Father's House

At the center of the heart of the Father is Family. We are above all else the Family of God; Brothers and Sisters, Fathers and Sons, Mothers and Daughters, living out life together in the covenant of a blood relationship, the blood of Christ. It is in the place of community that we are empowered to live out the authentic gospel of Christ, entering deep into intentional discipleship, accountability and teaching. The pure Church is committed to identifying the calling on each individual person's life and equipping them to the work of God that they are called to. One can find themselves at home in the house of prayer, being commissioned into the international mission field, or opening up their home to be an expression of the Father's House.

At the center, we express the Fathers heart for family in a replicating house church movement that seeks sustainable transformation both within our Family and in our community. I believe this is what scripture reveals the original church to be.

Let's look at some examples:

Acts 8:3 *But Saul was ravaging **the church**, and entering **house** after **house**, he dragged off men and women and committed them to prison.*
Acts 2:2 *And suddenly there came from heaven a sound like a mighty rushing wind, and it filled the entire **house** where they were sitting.*
Acts 5:42 *And every day, in the temple and from **house** to **house**, they did not cease teaching and preaching Jesus as the Christ.*
Romans 16:5 *Greet also the **church in their house**. Greet my beloved Epaenetus, who was the first convert to Christ in Asia.*
1Corinthians 16:19 *The churches of Asia send you greetings. Aquila and Prisca, together with the **church in their house**, send you hearty greetings in the Lord.*
Colossians 4:15 *Give my greetings to the brothers at Laodicea, and to Nympha and the **church in <u>her</u> house.***

The early Church seamed to be almost entirely located in an organically linked and apostolicly governed network of house churches. Although it was not uncommon to have public preaching and ministering, even teaching and meeting in the synagogues, the core

DNA of the Church was found in the homes. This thought was the prevailing model until at least the third century where felt need to control and organize the church led to the hierarchical Catholic church that we can see today. The life giving organism of the Church was officially made into an organization.

In the last couple hundred years, God has been pouring out His Spirit in ways mirroring the early days of Pentecost. These sovereign moves of God have been restoring the Church back to His original plan. We can see this in the move back towards a personal relationship with God, mediated only by Jesus. The priesthood of all believers is being restored. The gifts are being poured out afresh. The five-fold ministry offices are being renewed.

We can also observe the importance of small groups, cell groups and communities growing. Though there has always been a remnant, with monastic communities and the like bearing much of the fruit of the Church through the dark ages. However, it was when God restored this on the main stream, starting with the Moravians and then expanding through the ministry of John Wesley until we saw the birth of what is now known as the first Great Awakening. Present day, almost any good church model will emphasize the importance of cell group, small group, or house church communities for true discipleship and transformation to take place. As a matter of fact, Mega Shift is a book almost entirely concerned with the recording of these house church/micro-church communities and how they are covering the earth through epicenters of modern day revival.

It is in the organic, Holy Spirit birthed and sustained home churches that I am seeing the true work of Jesus happening. I don't know how many times I have prayed for someone who was drug addicted and saw them "accept Jesus" and get delivered of demons, only to see them belligerent and twice as oppressed one week later. People can say the sinner's prayer, get healed or delivered, and not get discipled. Now I do not take any encounter with Jesus lightly, and I know that we are called to sow indiscriminately. Sometimes we are just planting seeds that get watered years later. However, we are ultimately called to make disciples, and I see this best walked out in intentional community.

A story of a good friend comes to mind... I met Annette for the first time on the streets. She was 24 years old with a 2 year old daughter, living homeless and addicted to heroin. Within a few minutes of talking to her, we were able to pray and call on the Lord for salvation. Annette was tearing up and praying with sincerity as the Holy Spirit moved on her life. I gave her some contact information and then parted ways. I know Annette wanted to be free, but within a day she was back to the same life, playing with the fire of hard drugs. Just a short few weeks later she was being rushed to the hospital after a heavy overdose of heroin.

Another man named Kawika met us the 5th of July. The night before he had been in a fight, been arrested, and left with a mean black eye. We reached out to him and immediately brought him into our home. We quickly learned that he had been in jail for the last ten years! This was not uncommon to have drug dealers, rapists, felons, and addicts sleep on the floor next to us. However, Kawika was particularly volitile and even nearly assulted my little brother Chad, who, only 16 at the time, had deleted all of Kawika's gangsta rap music on his ipod and replaced it with all worship music. Ultimately, through patient endurance, the working of the Holy Spirit, and discipleship, Kawika became sober and softened to the point of tears in most 6am prayer meetings. A few months into his stay, Kawika brought in a new friend to the girls house church. This friend was recovering from a drug overdose and detoxing hard. I recognized this woman. Her name was Annette.

Annette spent the first week of her stay at a house church sick, tossing and turning, sweating and crying as the girls took turns covering her in prayer and looking after her as she kicked crystal meth and heroin. Since then we have seen many miraculously and instantly delivered from this drug and others. However, for Annette it was a daily struggle. What is important is that through presence of God centered community, Annette remained sober and grew in the Lord. As I write this, it was just last night that I heard the familiar sound of Annette's daughter Moana laughing at yet another house church meeting.

I praise God for the ministry of these women. So many have come to the knowledge of the love of their Savior through our women leaders. I fully embrace them, as does scripture. I embrace all the scriptures, husband being head of the wife, women being grown up in respectful submission, and all the rest. These serve God ordained purposes and give life when properly applied. But they are not contradictory. In fact, most of the recorded house Church leaders in the early church were women! There were also women prophetesses(Miriam, Huldah, Anna) and women judges/rulers(Debra) all the way from Israel down through the New Testament (Ex. 15:20, Judg.4:4, 2Kings22:14, 2Chr.34:22, Neh.6:14, Is.

8:3, Luke 2:36). After all, it does say in Acts 2:17 that, "In the last days it shall be, God declares, that I will pour out my Spirit on all flesh, and your sons and your daughters shall prophesy..." Ephesians 2:20 tells us that the foundation of this Church is to be the Apostles and Prophets. Sounds like women made the biblical cut for leadership to me.

Ok. Where were we. Oh yes. Caring for the broken hearted, the sick, the hungry, the poor in spirit and the lost. We aim to be the embodiment of the heart of the Father for a lost and hurting world. I don't care what age you are. It makes no difference your gender or race. God wants to use you as a chosen vessel of love.

House of Prayer

God came crashing into the Temple and shook things up to wake us up to this one very important reality... We need to pray! Everything we do must be out of a place of day and night prayer. Jesus lives forever to make intercession and I want to be like my Daddy! We are called to be a kingdom of priests, but as those who minister to HIM before all else. The churches need to have more confidence in His Spirit for salvation than all of our fleshly avenues and programs. The Bible exhorts us to pray constantly. Can you imagine the prayer meetings we would have if every believer was in constant day and night prayer? We wouldn't need charismatic speakers coming in and stirring us up. We would be yearning for those around us to come into agreement with the cries already on our heart!

Somehow prayer has become a controversial subject now days. My friend recently publicly said that all "contending prayer" is faithless and striving and is even worse than being an atheist. My response is that Jesus was not an atheist in the garden of Gethsemane. And when Jesus rose up from praying so hard that his capillaries were literally bursting, dripping blood down his face, there he found his church asleep. When Jesus calls us to pray, it is not always just soaking in his presence. There are many views and types of prayer, and many of them very important. I believe in communion with His Spirit, with chatting with God as our friend, I believe in making our lives a prayer and in soaking prayer. I also believe in the travail that leaves you groaning with birth pains, tarrying in the city to birth a move of Holy Spirit. Praying spontaneously and in the Spirit are of utmost importance. Likewise, going out to a certain spot in a customary fashion and time, and having times of communal prayer are all foundational to a healthy christian walk. You might be wondering how this happens, how do you pray without ceasing, in the spirit, in travail, spending time soaking and as a friend. It might take your whole life? Well it is true. God is not looking for a part time lover, He wants your life.

Every move of God and man of God has its beginning in prayer. I have never seen a man used by God who did not pray first. The Church was literally birthed in prayer, and is continually so. I know in my own life I have constantly evaluated the road in which I have traveled and set up markers to guide my way. I have found two areas that mark my "epic" seasons, the times that were exceptionally filled with the supernatural inbreakings of the Kingdom of God, and I have found they are **Prayer and Fasting**, paired with the **Ministry to the poor** (giving alms).

For All Nations

Anyone that is experiencing a legitimate move of the Holy Spirit will always bear the fruit of souls saved into the Kingdom. Scripture overwhelmingly reveals that when God shows up, there are thousands added to their numbers daily! The Church needs to press in to God for

His Presence, and when He comes they need to hit the streets in Power!

We talk about another student led missions movement, but we really need a new Holy Spirit led missions movement. The Church is going to tarry unto an inundation of power that would absolutely confound the world with the reality of Christ Jesus. We need to press in to a revelation of God's love that would so compel us, and of His Holy Ghost that would so empower us that we could not stay inside. I refuse to sit in a room full of cancer patients with the cure hidden in my glove box. The rate of full time clergy in America is almost 100 times as high as the international rate. If you just hop on Google for a few minutes and look up missionary statistics, you will be amazed. It seems we all feel that "someone else" will receive the call or do the job. The word of God is clear in its mission and game plan. Go to all the nations, preach to every soul, *then* Jesus will return. Do you long for your redeeming bridegroom King! If we love Him, then we will love His lost bride. If we want Him to come receive the reward of His suffering, we will preach the Gospel all over the world.

I do believe in urban missions. I understand and value the mission fields of the secular and christian universities, the first world marketplace, and even the western american church as a legitimate mission field. Many of my close friends are called to these areas as well. We have seen real outpourings on these campuses and in the secular workplaces, yet they carried this uncompromised message. Loren Cunningham once said in a meeting that "You are either a missionary or a mission field," and I couldn't agree more. While the mission field is vast here in our comfortable suburbia, God is still not wavering from His call. There *IS* something on location, and God has called us to go. In the words of famous musician Keith Green, "It should be the exception if you stay."

A few years back I had a friend who was struggling with his calling. He did not hear God tell him where to go. We sit on our couches in between commercial breaks and ask God if He would maybe like us to go somewhere or do something.   I told him to pick the darkest, most unreached place in the world and tell God that if he didn't show up and tell him not to, he was going to go there! See if that doesn't change your prayer life.

Room for Jesus

Behold, how good and pleasant it is when
brothers dwell together in unity! It is like the
precious oil on the head, running down on the
beard, on the beard of Aaron, running down on
the collar of his robes! It is like the dew of
Hermon, which falls on the mountains of Zion!
For there the LORD has commanded the
blessing, life forevermore. ~Psalm 133:1-3

God loves community. He has within Himself a
communion of the trinitarian nature. It is in the very
center of the heart of God to dwell together with man.
In the Old Testament we see that God so longs to be with
us that the God of the universe asked us to build Him a
little house that He might dwell in it. Since the beginning
God has been looking for a home with man.

Most christians are very excited for Heaven, and
rightfully so! We so dearly long for a home with the

Father. Many even just endure this life anxiously awaiting their room in the Father's house. The question I pose is amidst your desire for a room in God's house, do you have room for God in yours? We want God to open up His heavenly home to us, but we deny him entry into ours. Certainly I am talking about the temple of our bodies, in which God desires to have communion with our spirits. But how can we say we have given him the spiritual things if we still hold tightly to our physical house?

In 2 Kings 4 the Shunammite Woman welcomes Elisha, the great prophet and man of God, into her home every time he comes by. She even goes out of her way to construct a spare bedroom just so that the ambassador of God can be welcomed in whenever. She was so blessed by this that she was given a son, and when he died, Elisha raised him from the dead. It was her act of love that released the power for the first recorded dead raising in history!

Eternal life is certainly the great hope of the Gospel. It is the pearl of great price worth selling everything just to buy. John defines eternal life as knowing Jesus, and Jesus would say to know me in the least of these. It is so easy for the Church to say, "we love God," but if we can't love the person in front of us, who we can see and touch, how can we say we love God. In Psalm 133 we see that the Blessing of Eternal Life and the oil of His Holy Spirit are all commanded to reside in the place of community. "How good and pleasant when brothers dwell together in unity," the scriptures say. Unity is easy at a distance, but God is looking for those who are willing to *dwell together* in unity. " *For there the LORD has commanded the blessing, life forevermore." Ps. 133*

For thirty three years Jesus lived, then He died, and then three days later He rose again. The unique and unifying factor of all the accounts of the appearances of Jesus after His resurrection was that He was hard to recognize. Even those that had spent much time with Jesus were unable to recognize Him with their eyes and just felt a burning in their hearts (Luke 24). In His time with us on earth, Jesus encouraged us that whatever we do to the least of these we do to Him. It is exciting that we never know when we might be entertaining an angel, but how much more when we are among the poor and broken hearted. Sometimes we may be entertaining Jesus Himself without even realizing it!

There are many examples I could share on this note. I remember vividly this one time, with my friend who we will just call Jessica. I was ministering on the streets with a friend that was doing a report on the homeless my Junior year of college. He wanted to understand more about the subculture of ocean beach and knew I spent much of my time down there. As we were wrapping up and heading to grab some food, we were approached by a beautiful woman named Jessica. Jessica was probably in her early thirties, but she already had wrinkling and spotted skin as someone twice her age. She was asking for money, but it was obvious by her shaking and scratching that it was just for drugs. Instead of giving her money, we insisted that she join us for dinner at her favorite sit down restaurant in town. As our conversation progressed, we learned about Jessica's childhood. We learned of the brokenness she grew up in and the life of sex and drugs that she grew up in. Even now I feel the ache that was in my heart, crying out to save the little girl trapped in this decaying body. We wanted desperately to minister to her, but God was there to minister to us. When my friend got up to use the bathroom, and it was just me and Jessica, the presence of God came so heavy. All of a sudden I looked in Jessica's eyes and they were full of warmth, love and light. She began to speak, "Paul, I love you. I love it when you spend time with me. I have great plans for you. I have called you and will use you mightily." I was no longer eating dinner with Jessica. As I began to weep, Jesus told me of His love and His plans for me. The best prophetic word's I've ever received have always come from Him.

There is such an opportunity available. Jesus has chosen to reside among those whose calendars are never booked, and who are the most willing to spend some quality time.

Matt. 25:34-40 *Then the King will say to those on his right, 'Come, you who are blessed by my Father, inherit the kingdom prepared for you from the foundation of the world. For I was hungry and you gave me food, I was thirsty and you gave me drink, I was a stranger and you welcomed me, I was naked and you clothed me, I was sick and you visited me, I was in prison and you came to me.' Then the righteous will answer him, saying, 'Lord, when did we see you hungry and feed you, or thirsty and give you drink? And when did we see you a stranger and welcome you, or naked and clothe you? And when did we see you sick or in prison and visit you?' And the King will answer them, 'Truly, I say to you, as you did it to one of the least of these my brothers, you did it to me.'*

Everyday that we say with our mouths we love Jesus we have a choice: we can leave Him hungry on the street, or we can love Him as He first loved us by giving our lives for Him.   Will Jesus say He knows us? I have not found a tangible way to determine. Yet I know that if you ask around the poor in San Diego, many will know our name.

God's Government

"And he will turn the hearts of fathers to their children and the hearts of children to their fathers, lest I come and strike the land with a decree of utter destruction."
~Malachi 4:6

God is a good Father who sent His only Son with the Spirit of Adoption to adopt a bunch of kids, to raise up a Bride to marry her Husband. Sounds like family. God has given us family as a prophetic insight into the heart of Heaven, that we might know love. All of our lives point toward the great marriage of the Lamb. Our journey begins with being brought home into the Father's love. For God, family is more about love than it is about blood. We tend to think that our personal blood family is priority and it does have a special place. We just need to remember that God gave His only son to adopt a bunch of kids that captured His heart. It is not just about bloodlines and genealogies. Paul actually told us to get over endless genealogies. It is about brotherly love and closeness in heart, in mind, in time, and often proximity. Jesus said those who do the will of the Father are His family. We need family unity in proximity. We need a Church that is willing to spend time with each other and love each other amidst doing the will of the Father. How good and pleasant it is when Husbands and Wives, when children and parents, when preachers and parishioners, when brothers and sisters dwell together in unity. There are countries all over the world that understand family better than America. In Mexico it is not uncommon to live with three or four generations and two or three other bloodlines all in one house. There are villages all around the world that understand those around them to be their family. Even in the Gospels we see a Church of locality which is identified by their region, such as the "Church in Ephesus" or the "Church in Corinth" etc. So while we are brothers with all in Christ, there is still your local family which will have its center with your household, then your local church body, and expanding to your greater tribe or denomination, and coming together in honor with the whole Bride. Many people want a pure and spotless Bride with great revival coming to the churches or even just their local church. As for me, I would lament to ever see revival come to my city and miss my wife and kids. Let revival start with our homes and overflow into our world.

Godly Honor and Submission

We don't understand the Kingdom of God in America. Probably because we don't have a king. The Kingdom of God where we call Jesus Lord is one of right alignment and submission to the rule of God, something like the Government of God. It is through this Government that God executes justice and releases His goodness to all the people in His land.   One of the most tragic sins has swept through two of the most important area's of our lives, our churches and our families. This sin is rebellion. We can attribute this to the spirit of Jezebel, Ahab, Feminism, or whatever else. All of these have lent their destructive hands, but we each have an individual decision to make. Is God going to be ruling Lord or not? Many say with their lips "Lord, Lord," but when their opinions of how things should be differ from what God has said, who wins? If God says to do one thing and we do another, He was not given Lordship... we were in Rebellion.

People are born into rebellion, and we all need to deal with it at some point. Rebellion can't be cast out, it has to be repented of. Only then will we see the lasting freedom we are looking for. We cast off the false freedom and the fear of control in favor of godly honor and submission. It is in this place that we find "the Kingdom of God" coming in our lives, and we eat the fruit of His good rule. And as Jesus said, "the kingdom of God is amongst us." God has commanded us concerning these things.

Heb. 13:17 *Obey your leaders and* **submit** *to them, for they are keeping watch over your souls, as those who will have to give an account. Let them do this with joy and not with groaning, for that would be of no advantage to you.*

Eph. 5:22 *Wives,* **submit** *to your own husbands, as to the Lord.*

Eph. 5:24 *Now as the church* **submits** *to Christ, so also wives should* **submit** *in everything to their husbands.*

Col. 3:18 *Wives,* **submit** *to your husbands, as is fitting in the Lord.*

Ex. 20:12   *"**Honor** your father and your mother, that your days may be long in the land that the LORD your God is giving you.*

1Tim. 5:17 *Let the elders who rule well be considered worthy of double **honor**, especially those who labor in preaching and teaching.*

Please read the scriptures! My commentary is the condiments, but the sustaining meal is always the Word! I teach this because I am commanded to and because I trust Jesus knew what He was doing when He designed His Kingdom. I believe that when I trust Him and His good plans, that it will be the best possible option.

I recognize that there has been perversion of this in history, and lament on behalf of both cultures and churches that have used these concepts for selfish gain and control. Whether it is in the home or in the church, I understand that oppression has taken place in the name of "submission." I think that both husbands and church leaders need to take a serious look at the responsibility they carry, and remember that they are not only double honored, but doubly accountable to the Lord.

In the end, this is God's design. It doesn't matter what you or I think. Jesus is Lord. And He is also totally good. The truth is that submission is actually very life giving and is conducive to order, which promotes growth. As Christians, we are firstly submitted to Jesus as our Lord. From that place, we submit to one another as Christians, recognizing that Jesus humbled himself as a servant, and the He has commanded us to submit to those He has put in our lives as onto the Lord. Jesus said that we cannot say that we love Him who we can't see, if we cannot love those around us. Similarly, can we say we submit to Jesus as Lord when we do not submit to those He says He has placed in our lives as His representative?

Ultimately, we need to trust God as our redeemer. We must be faithful to His commands and believe that He is the rewarder of the just. It would do us good to remember David, and how he submitted to even his wicked ruler Saul. God rewarded him and lifted him up. Our only other option is to sin by going into rebellion due to a lack of faith, not trusting that God rewards those who follow Him.

1Sam. 15:23   *"For rebellion is as the sin of divination,*

And insubordination is as iniquity and idolatry.
Because you have rejected the word of the LORD,
He has also rejected you from being king." (NASB)

When we become insubordinate we say that we don't trust God, but that we could do a better job through our ideas or ways. This is idolatry and sin because it doesn't proceed from faith in God, but rather faith in Self. Rebellion is witchcraft because it always seeks to manipulate others to will against God in favor of their ways, which originate from their flesh, and not the Word.

The heart of God for right authority is not to suppress, but to to empower. True authority creates a place of safety and order that promotes growth and excels us into destiny. The psalms tell us His rod and staff comfort us. While these tools are used to discipline and direct us, they are the same things that drive the enemy out of our flock and allows us to graze peacefully in the green pastures of His Kingdom.

Catching the Fire

"I came to cast **fire** on the earth, and
would that it were already kindled!"

~Jesus (Luke 12:49)

One night, in the spring of 2011, I was seeking
direction with the Lord. I was also looking for a hotel
room for my friend and I to stay at until we could find
him a more permanent solution (which we did soon after
in one of our house churches). In the morning, I awoke
from a dream that would altar the direction of my life. In
the dream I was galloping up a wide mountain path
toward the summit. Gaining speed toward the peak, I
eventually came upon a mountain ledge wall that reared
my horse up to an immediate halt. As I jumped off my
horse, I noticed the wall had a ancient drawing of my

horse rearing up while I got off to go down a narrow road. I looked to my left and saw a narrow path going down past a tree and then down along the side of the mountain. As I walked towards it I got spat on by a black bird, which I rebuked in the name of Jesus, causing it to fly away. I kept walking past the tree, and as soon as I began the journey down the narrow path, I saw a golden yellow bird. In the dream I immediately knew it was a yellow canary, and out of its mouth came a booming voice which said,

" **I have given you a little seed. Go swiftly and spread it and I will start wild fires everywhere you go!**"

Now for those of you who are spiritual, I will let you discern the details and fullness of what God was saying, but allow me to key in on some profound details. The wider road may allow you to travel quickly and you may even be heading in the right direction, but it will only take you so far. There is an ancient path that has long since been written of in the holy scriptures which the devil does not want you to find.

The path may be narrow in a more challenging direction, but it is marked by the tree. The tree is both life and death. It is the tree by the river of life that has healing in its wings, and it is the cross where our sin and flesh is crucified. It is in this place that we meet God.

It is not everyday that I hear the booming audible voice of God, in a dream or not! I believe there is an authority and a depth on this revelation that is timely for us now. Stranger yet is the mode of delivery, a yellow canary?! Now not being much of a bird person myself, I knew it had to be the Lord telling me something. So I did a little research and this is what I found; Yellow Canaries are seed spreading birds. This means that they eat a lot of fruit and then scat-ter it throughout whatever territory that they fly through. I also found that these Yellow Canaries are among the youngest of weening birds. This means that God is releasing seed scatterers at a younger age than ever. Where other birds can take months or years to be mature enough to go out on their own, this breed is released in just a few short weeks! God is raising up thousands in this generation equipped with the earth shaking power of the gospel, and it is packaged in the tinniest of seeds.

We need to come to a place of freedom and confidence in the Holy Spirit where we are able to release people into the work of ministry like never before. We are in such a time as we are and cannot afford ten years for a doctorate and years in the corporate ministry ladder before finally being released into God's destiny. While ministry coverings, godly submission, etc. are all valid and valuable aspects to the kingdom, our ministries and mentors need to come to a place of security in God where we are able to empower instead of imprison.

Another amazing thing about God's message is His use of imagery. Both spreading seed and starting fires can teach us a ton about what God is wanting to do in this hour. In the Bible, we see Jesus constantly using organic things in His analogies to the Kingdom of God. Specifically, He says in 5 different places that the Kingdom of God is like a mustard seed, in Matt.13:31, Matt.17:20, Mark 4:31, Luke 13:19, and luke 17:6. Jesus tells us that the mustard seed is the smallest of all the seeds, and that when it is sown among the forest it may seem inconsequential and remain invisible for a time, but it will eventually overtake the forest. If you were to cast the seed throughout a concrete jungle, it would take root in the cracks and trickle into the lowest and most hidden places. As the rains come, these tiny invisible seeds would spring up roots that would break up even the hardest foundations and send even the biggest skyscrapers toppling over. Jesus tells us with faith like a mustard seed we could move the mountains. These little seeds spring up into giant trees that give shade to, guess what, Birds! God is so clever.

I believe what God is saying is that we need to return to the ancient roots of an organic Church. One that springs up from the cracks from the planting of the tiniest seeds. This is an army of little people daring to be small in the middle of a giant forest, believing that God plus me equals the majority. This does not leave room for us to claim it, label it, or control it. Like a fire that you started that caught some local brush and took off, it has become out of your control. Every move of God is able to move as long and as far as we are willing to keep our hands out of it. As soon as we try to fence in all the trees into our orchard or make sure the flock ends up in our pasture, we contain and necessarily limit what God was trying to do. We need to be ok with spreading the seed of the kingdom and watching it grow into a tree with our God given DNA without trying to claim the tree. We need to acknowledge that the Kingdom belongs to the King.

In my own life I have seen this work itself out practically. Others have sown seeds into my life of what missional communities and the raw movement of God's love looks like, and it has grown into a tree that gives shade to all kinds of life. As our tree grows and birds and animals feed on the fruit, the seed is scattered. We have seen many other similar trees sprout up. Many of them have chosen to associate themselves as a part of our family and really embrace our church's structure and identity. Others have called themselves other things or express themselves in other ways, and we have come to embrace this as well. Any good dad wants his kids to find their own identity. He would only create division if he tried to force his personality on his children.

I find great joy in reading about communities of God in the newspaper that have grown organically out of even the tiniest seed. We are watching as communities seeking the purity of Jesus and loving the poor in power spring up all across california, the states and beyond. This is the fresh anointing that is available today. God is sweeping through our cities. His Spirit is searching hearts and homes, looking for all that He could use. His anointing is the person of the Holy Spirit and is not inanimate. He has eyes and ears. The anointing is listening for the weak, yet daring prayers. He is looking for the one. For the ones He could show himself strong and victorious through, to a world so desperately in need.

ABOUT THE AUTHOR

Paul Krause gave everything to God at 16 when he was sovereignly visited by Jesus while detained in solitary confinement. Paul started his first church when he was only 20. After baptizing a number of people in the pacific ocean, the need for a place to disciple the newly converted arose. Not wanting to burden the church, Paul has started a number of businesses from a retail/tea company named "Realitea"(newrealitea.com) and InTheCity Travel Guides(inthecity.co). Paul and his wife Katie just had their first daughter, Charis and see family as the most important thing they do. To learn more or invite paul to speak, you can visit CalledOutMin.com.

Recommended Reading

Church
Megashift by James Rutz
Culture of Honor by Danny Silk
Revolution by George Barna

Christian Living
When Heaven Invades Earth by Bill Johnson
Pursuit of the Holy by A.W. Tozer
Growing in the Prophetic by Mike Bickle
Ecstatic Prophecy by Stacey Campbell
Breaking Free by Beth Moore

Biographies
Visions Beyond the Veil by H.A. Baker
Heavenly Man by Brother Yun
Like a Mighty Rushing Wind by Mel Tari
Compelled by Love by Heidi Baker

Websites of Interest

Paul's Ministries
www.CalledOutMin.com
www.rosesforroyalty.com

Paul's Business
www.InTheCitySanDiego.com
www.InTheCity.co
www.NewRealitea.com

Other Resources
www.IrisMin.com
www.iBethel.org
www.xpmedia.com

Called Out

www.CalledOutMin.com